CALLIGRAPHY PRACTICE WORKBOOK

This Book Belongs To

www.ingramcontent.com/pod-product-compliance
Lightning Source LLC
Chambersburg PA
CBHW081516220526
45467CB00010B/2940
* 9 7 8 1 7 1 2 3 7 9 2 5 7 *